The Bell, The Clapper, And The Cord: Wit And Witticism

Large Type Edition

**Published by
The National Federation
of the Blind**

Table of Contents

Introduction

I was first elected President of the National Federation of the Blind in 1968. Shortly after that I began sending cassette tape recordings to be played for our members at their local monthly chapter meetings. From the very beginning, I have included a touch of humor at the end of these tapes. I did this because these "Presidential Messages" were always filled with the serious problems of blindness, and I wanted to share these jokes and funny stores with my friends...to take our minds off the problems of blindness and to lighten the day's burden with a little fun.

Before long individual blind people began sending me jokes and funny stories to share with their brothers and sisters in the NFB family across the country, and these items became a traditional part of our local monthly meetings.

Many members of the NFB have wished for a compilation of "Presidential Message" jokes and funny stories. This book—*THE BELL, THE CLAPPER, AND THE CORD*—is the answer to that wish. I hope that when you read this book, you will smile and forget your daily problems ... even for just a few minutes.

Kenneth Jernigan
President Emeritus

Why Large Type

The type size in this book is 14 point for two important reasons: One, because typesetting of 14 point or larger complies with federal standards for the printing of materials for visually impaired readers, and we wanted to show you exactly what type size is necessary for people with limited sight.

The second reason is that many of our friends and supporters have asked us to print our paperback books in 14-point type so they too can easily read them. Many people with limited sight do not use Braille. We hope that by printing this book in a larger type than customary, many more people will be able to benefit from it.

Kenneth Jernigan, *President Emeritus*
National Federation of the Blind

Conditions of Employment

We live in the space age. The other day somebody said to me, "Do you know what astronauts eat?"

"No," I said.

"Launch meat," he answered.

If athletes have athlete's foot, then what do astronauts have?

Mistle toe, of course.

I heard a man being introduced the other day like this:

This fellow must be a farmer because he's outstanding in his field.

I have a couple of quickies for you. Do you know when the cook is mean?

Why, the cook is mean when he beats the eggs and whips the cream.

Or, did you hear about the girl named Rose Bush who went into the bee keeping business and got hives?

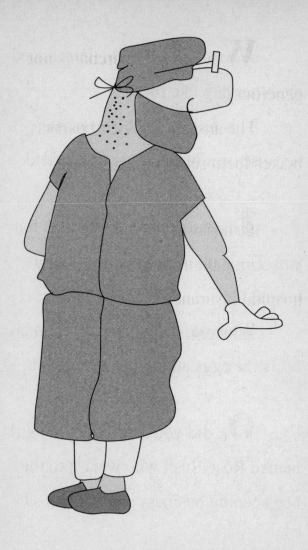

Why are fish merchants not generous?

The answer is: Their business makes them selfish.

The surgeon said to the stubborn patient who wouldn't buy hospital insurance:

All right, suture self.

Did you hear about the man
who tried to run a symphony and did
such a bad job they decided to
electrocute him?

But they couldn't, he was such a
poor conductor.

Did you hear about Dr. Duck?
Well, he was a real quack.

Take this one...

Why is it that the hearing of
people who work on the railroad is
different from other people's hearing?

Why, because they have engine ears.

Did you hear about the student archaeologist who found his career in ruins?

Who has the easiest job in the world?

Easy, a candlemaker—he only has to work on wick ends.

I find people flooding me now with all kinds of stories which they think would be suitable, for instance:

Do you know that a lazy butcher is called a meat loafer?

Why was it that in the old West they used manicurists to build gallows?

Well, that's because, of course, manicurists are expert in dealing with hangnails.

What is a leisure suit?

Well, it's a case handled by a lawyer in his spare time.

How about the dermatologist who started his business from scratch?

Do you know about the cross-eyed teacher?

She had trouble with her pupils.

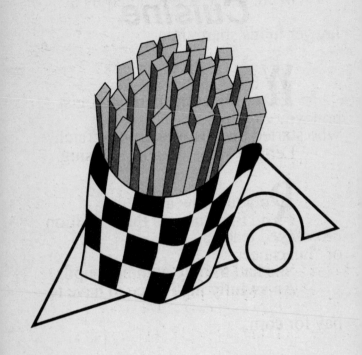

Delectable Cuisine

What is the recipe for honeymoon salad?

Lettuce alone without dressing.

And then there is the definition of "buccaneer."

An awfully high price to have to pay for corn.

Two carrots were going down the street, and one of 'em got run over by a car. So, the first carrot took the other to the hospital and waited outside. After a while the doctor came out and said:

Well, I got good news and bad news for you 'bout your friend, the other carrot.

The good news is, it's gonna live.

The bad news is, I'm afraid it's gonna be a vegetable for the rest of its life.

Have you heard about the new drink? Local hardware stores are selling it.

You take milk of magnesia, vodka, and orange juice, to make a Phillips screwdriver.

Do you know why watermelons have water in them?

Why, because they're planted in the spring.

Did you hear about the wife who said when she got home from the party:

"My, those cookies were hard!"

The husband replied: "I suppose that's why the hostess said, 'Take your pick.'"

Do you know what happens when a dog breaks into a chicken house?

You get pooched eggs.

Halloweeners

The following three jokes are very specialized and seem to deserve a category to themselves. Children from three to ninety-three may wish to review them in late October.

Where do you take a ghost to get him repaired if he backs into a power lawn mower?

You take him to a liquor store, for that's where they retail spirits!

How do you make a witch scratch?

You take away its *w*.

You know that all barbecuers love the "grate" outdoors, and also, I wonder if you know what you get when you take the middle out of a hot dog during the latter part of October.

Why, you get a hollow weener.

17

Creatures Great and Small

Do you know what you get when there are thirty rabbits in a row marching backwards?

You have a receding hairline.

Somebody sent me a story the other day—I think it was a ten-year-old boy who said:

Do you know what happens to a sheep when he goes to get his hair cut?

He goes to the baa baa shop.

Do you know the definition of melancholy?

It's a dog that eats cantaloupes.

Or, do you know why cows wear bells?

Their horns don't work.

Did you hear about the two silkworms who got into a race and ended up in a tie?

Why did the turtle cross the road?

To get to the shell station!

Did you know that during the American Revolution the Americans used chickens to do sentry duty? From which we get the term, "chicken catch a Tory."

Why did the crow light on the telephone wire?

He wanted to make a long distance caw.

Do you know what kind of dog is best able to keep time?

A watch dog.

Where do bees get their transportation?

At the buzz stop.

What happens when you sterilize a cow?

>She's decaffeinated.

By the way, the other day somebody asked me if I knew what you'd call a sleeping bull.

>I told 'em: No.

>And he told me it was a bulldozer.

I call my little dog Hardware because when he hears his name he bolts for the door.

Did you hear about the cat who ate cheese and sat by the mouse hole with baited breath?

Do you know why the farmer called his pig Ink?

Because he always kept running out of the pen.

A Special Kind of Wisdom

Did you know about the young lady who went to the barber shop and was distressed?

Did you know that old mufflers never die, they're just exhausted?

What colors should you paint the sun and the wind?

The sun rose, and the wind blue.

It reminded me of the old Henry Morgan days. I used to race out from the dining room at the Tennessee School for the Blind in order to listen to Henry Morgan on the radio. And he once said that the weather forecast for expectant fathers was son and heir.

I'm sure you know that seven days in bed makes one weak.

Perhaps you've heard of the young man whose father died and left him his entire collection of antique clocks.

It seems the young man spent the rest of his life winding up his father's estate.

Why does it take longer to run from second base to third base, than from first base to second base?

Because there's a shortstop in between.

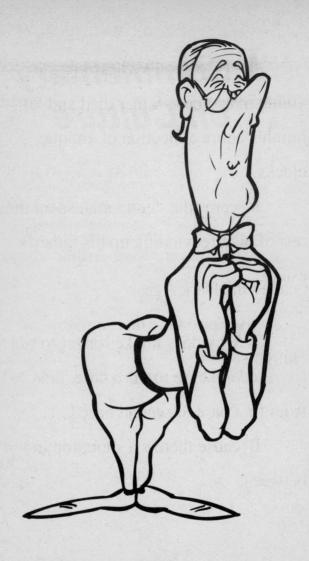

A Commentary on Culture

Why were King Arthur's days called the Dark Ages?

Because they had so many knights.

Inflation is really getting bad. As a matter of fact it is so bad it's not just that the economic crunch is all over the world.

No, it's worse than that. It's universal—even the moon is getting down to its last quarter.

Somebody said: Is our greatest problem ignorance or apathy?

To which the individual replied: I don't know and I don't care.

Do you know what you'd call a butcher's dance?

A meatball.

Did you hear about the Eskimo who was stabbed with an icicle and died of cold cuts?

Presidential Riddles

What do you get when you cross a statement with a coat hanger?

Why, you get a suspended sentence.

Why did the wagon train stop in the middle of the desert?

It had Injun trouble.

What did the hat say to the hat rack?

You stay here, I'll go on ahead.

Why doesn't the paper on the desk move?

Because it's stationery.

What's worse than raining cats and dogs?

Hailing buses.

Can you tell me when baseball was mentioned in the Bible?

Well, Abraham made a sacrifice, Rebecca went to the well with a pitcher, and then the book of Genesis starts by telling what happened in the big-inning.

Why in church do we say Amen instead of Awomen?

Because we sing hymns, not hers.

Why can't a bicycle stand upright alone?

The answer is: It's two tired.

Why do you go to bed at night?

Because the bed won't come to you.

Do you know what Cinderella said to the photographer?

Some day my prints will come.

What happens when a rattlesnake marries a mortician?

Well, they get wedding gifts marked "hiss" and "hearse."

Life in the Fast Lane

Have you ever thought about all the events and components that make up a lifetime? Doubtless, you'll view things differently with respect to children, parenting, and life in general following your perusal of this section.

There was the man who heard that three-fourths of all accidents happen within ten miles of home, so he moved.

What kind of wood do you use to build a cow shed?

Cattle logs.

What is the greatest worldwide use of cowhide?

To hold cows together.

Why is it illegal for cats to be tried by a jury of their peers?

The reason is obvious.

It would be purr jury.

I call my dog Ginger. Does Ginger bite?

No, Ginger snaps.

What did the man say as he gave his dog his dinner?

"Bone appetite."

Why are the heart of an oak tree and a hound's tail alike?

They're both the farthest from the bark.

A dog is such a lovable creature because it wags its tail instead of its tongue.

Why did the three-legged dog return to Dodge City?

He wanted to find the fellow who shot his paw.

A dog is a man's best friend, and it should be. Consider. I work hard every day. I work like a dog. That's the reason I'm always dog-tired. But he never works hard. He's lazy as a dog.

When I go out on a date, I always put on the dog.

If I owe people money, they dog my footsteps.

In times of conflict, the dogs of war are unleashed.

Meanwhile, those who are young have puppy love.

There are bird dogs, watch dogs, hot dogs, and underdogs.

And when I'm feeling oppressed, I say I lead a dog's life.

Did you hear about the flea circus?

The dog came by and stole the show.

What's better than a talking dog?

Why a spelling bee.

What happened to the pelican who stuck his head into the light socket?

He got an electric bill.

On what day are more babies born than any other day of the year?

And of course, the answer is on Labor Day.

What did one ink spot say to the other?

My dad is in the pen; I don't know how long the sentence is.

Why does it get so hot in a stadium after a baseball game?

All of the fans have left.

What do you do when the bases are loaded?

Well, you sober them up or you replace them with baritones.

Did you hear about the football player who went to the telephone store and bought a wide receiver?

It cost him $29.75, so he gave the clerk $30 and got a quarterback.

How is golf like taxes?

Well, you drive hard to get to the green, and then you wind up in the hole.

What did the fisherman give to the Internal Revenue Service at tax time?

Why, his net income.

Why did the old lady put wheels on her rocking chair?

So she could rock and roll.

When is a car not a car?

When it turns into a driveway.

Did you hear about the
magician who went down the street
and turned into a grocery store?

Why do hummingbirds always
hum?

Because they don't know the
words.

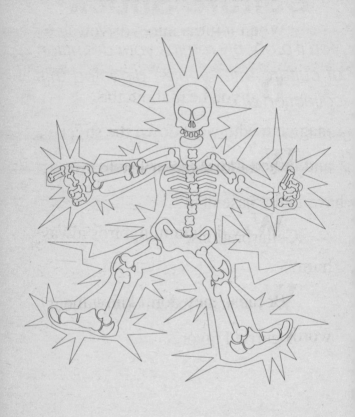

Culture Shock

You'll probably rethink your definition of culture after you've digested this collection of data.

What kind of parties do you have in the basement?

Cellarbrations.

What is an Indian compliment?

A curried favor.

Why are long distance calls in Persia so expensive?

Why, because they're Persian to Persian.

This is what the German fellow said when the thief snatched his toupee.

"Mine hair!"

Why do Eskimos wash in Tide?

Because it's too cold to wash out Tide.

Where does the snowman keep
his money?

In the Snow Bank.

Those who live in the Sahara
Desert are almost never hungry
because of the sand which is there.

Television is called a medium.
It isn't rare and it isn't well-done.

What is quicksilver?

Well, that is what the Lone
Ranger says when he's in a hurry.

A lady drove into a gas station. The attendant said, "Fill her up?"

The lady said, "I'd be tank full if you would."

This fine Protestant said to her minister, "Please pray for my pancreas."

The minister said, "Well, ma'am, we don't usually get so specific in our prayers."

And she said, "Oh, yes, you do. Last week you prayed for loose livers."

There was a man who wouldn't take his wife out to eat. He'd been told he shouldn't go out with married women.

When does a timid girl turn into a stone?
When she becomes a little boulder.

Somewhere Between the Barn and the Vegetable Patch

The history of humor wouldn't be complete without its references to vegetables, farm and zoo animals, and their activities. These may inspire some of your own contributions.

What did the one strawberry say to the other?

Look what a jam you got us into.

How do you fix a pumpkin?
With a pumpkin patch.

Why do melons have church
weddings?
The answer is obvious.
They cantaloupe.

What do you get when you
cross a cantaloupe with Lassie?
A melon collie baby.

What did the grape say when the elephant stepped on it?

It just let out a little whine.

What do you call a cow that enters your yard and eats your grass?

A lawn mooer.

What do you get when you cross a turtle and a cow?

A turtle-necked jersey.

Did you hear about the man who was working in the field and a load of cotton dropped on him?

He was baleful.

What do you call a male deer who is just crazy about a female deer?

You call him a doe nut.

What do you get when you cross a turkey with an octopus?

Enough drumsticks for everybody.

What does a baby ear of corn call its father?

Of course, Pop Corn.

Why did the farmer's wife chase the chickens out of the yard?

They were using fowl language.

How do you know when chickens are possessed?

Well, you know when you get deviled eggs.

Why is the change in your pocket called chicken feed?

Because it's such a poultry sum.

Why should you be discrete on a farm?

Because corn has ears, potatoes have eyes, and beans talk.

The Employee's Handbook

One wonders how this section will impact the 70 percent unemployment rate among blind persons in the United States, and if any of these offerings assist you in your job search, do let us know.

A secretary confused a food processor and a word processor and minced her words.

Did you hear about the secretary who always typed in lower case?

She simply couldn't shift for herself.

Why did all the janitors go on strike?

They wanted sweeping reforms.

Did you hear about the rock and roll boxer?

He would always punch people to the beat.

Did you hear about the man who was hired and fired by the circus in the same day?

He was a human cannon ball.

Why do pirates make good sopranos?

They are always hitting the high seas.

Why are policemen so strong?

Because they keep holding up traffic.

Did you hear about the burglars who drove up in a van to a museum and began stealing the paintings?

Trouble is when they got ready to leave, they couldn't make the van go.

Why did the bow-legged cowboy get fired?

Because he couldn't keep his calves together.

What's the difference between a dentist and a loyal New Yorker?

Well, a dentist yanks for the roots and a loyal New Yorker roots for the Yanks.

Some Things Never Change

There are certain laughter-evoking phrases and lines that have been around as long as many of us began sharing jokes among ourselves and our friends. The origin of some of these jokes cannot be attributed to the provider, so read and enjoy!

Why is a banana peel like a piano?

If you don't C sharp, you'll B flat.

If money does not grow on trees, then why do banks have branches?

A man who carries his watch in his back pocket will never be behind time.

You heard of the man who came home soaking wet and told his wife it was raining cats and dogs and he had to work hard to avoid stepping onto a poodle.

The man went into the restaurant and said, "Do you serve crabs here?"

And the waiter said, "Why, yes sir, we serve anybody here."

Why are scarecrows always winning awards?

Because they're outstanding in their field.

How do you communicate with a fish?

You drop him a line.

It's Academic

What did the volcano say to
the earthquake?

    It's not my fault.

Why is the sea so restless?

Because it has rocks in its bed.

When can you tell an ocean is
friendly?

    Of course, when it waves.

What is it that lies on the bottom of the ocean and shakes?

A nervous wreck.

What do you get when you cross a dinosaur and a termite?

Of course, dynamite.

Did you hear about the nuclear scientist?

He swallowed a uranium pill and got atomic ache.

What happens to a teacher who retires?

The teacher loses all his principals.

What did the English teacher call Santa's helpers?

Subordinate Clauses.

Healthful Hints

Medical terms have been defined and redefined throughout the history of Presidential Releases. Here are some offerings that may bring new meaning to the mystery of medical science.

A lot of women are lately getting an epidemic of the Egyptian flu.

They're becoming mummies.

Why did the little shoe have psychological problems?

Because its father was a loafer and its mother was a sneaker.

A man went to his psychiatrist and he said, "Sometimes I think I'm a tepee and sometimes I think I'm a wigwam."

The psychiatrist said, "Your problem is you're too tents."

Did you hear about the man who went to the doctor and said that he felt like a pair of curtains?

And the doctor said, "Come now, pull yourself together."

The man went to the doctor because every time he put on his hat, he heard music.

The doctor fixed everything.

He took the band out.

Why are carpet layers always so depressed?

People are always looking down on their work.

What do you put on a sick pig? Of course, oinkment.

What is the meaning of *dilate*? That's what happens to patients who live longer than expected.

And then there's the meaning of *barium*.

That's what you do with patients when they dilate.

For your Information

Primarily, people come to the National Federation of the Blind to discuss blindness. Often we learn other things as well, such as the following tidbits:

Did you hear about the ship that sailed from Taiwan with a cargo of yo-yos?

It sank 184 times.

Why did the golfer wear two pairs of pants?

Well, just in case he got a hole in one.

What do you call a broken boomerang?

A stick.

What is a fish's favorite tv show?

Name that tuna.

When is coffee like a bear?

When it's bruin.

National Federation of the Blind

You can help us spread the word…

…about our Braille Readers Are Leaders contest for blind schoolchildren, a project which encourages blind children to achieve literacy through Braille.

…about our scholarships for deserving blind college students.

…about Job Opportunities for the Blind, a program that matches capable blind people with employers who need their skills.

…about where to turn for accurate information about blindness and the abilities of the blind.

Most importantly, you can help us by sharing what you've learned about blindness in these pages with your family and friends. If you know anyone who needs assistance with the problems of blindness, please write:

Marc Maurer, President
1800 Johnson Street, Suite 300
Baltimore, Maryland 21230-4998
Your contribution is tax-deductible.